Ready for Science

Jane Glover
Milton Road Infants' School, Cambridge

David Glover
Lecturer in Science, Cambridgeshire College of Arts and Technology

This book belongs to

_____

I started it on

_____

I finished it on

_____

I am _____ years old

Illustrated by Clare Beaton

To Parents

All children are naturally curious about themselves and the world around them. They love to experiment with sand and water, to watch the birds and squirrels in the park or to invent fantastic machines. This series of books is specially designed to develop children's scientific knowledge and skills through activities that are fun and easy to do at home with everyday materials.

Science is an important part of the curriculum in today's primary schools. From the first year in the infant school, science activities are introduced to develop observation and problem-solving skills, as well as to stimulate children's curiosity about the world around them.

The content and level of the activities in this book follow closely the approach to science that your child is likely to meet when he or she first goes to school.

Sharing activities can be a very rewarding experience for parents as well as children. This book provides lots of opportunities to share your child's learning and to show that you value your child's ideas and discoveries.

How to use this book

Check the introduction and notes to the chosen activity and make sure that you have to hand all the materials you will need.

Read the instructions to your child and talk about the activity. Make sure that your child understands what to do.

Join in the activity – but try to let your child take the lead. Encourage your child to try things out and ask questions rather than immediately showing the child what to do.

Don't try to do too much at one time; one activity a session is enough for a child of 4-5 years.

Talk about the activity at every stage. Encourage your child to describe and discuss observations and discoveries as they are made. Don't expect children of this age to record answers in writing.

There are **notes** throughout the book to help you. On page 32 you will find a more detailed explanation of the ways in which these activities help your child's learning.

There is a pull-out **games board** in the centre of this book. Games are of particular value because they enable children to learn in an enjoyable way.

These activities have already been tried out and enjoyed by many children. We hope that you and your child will enjoy discovering science with them at home!

Jane & David Glover

The science gang

Tiger

Owl

Fred

Annie

Mix

Max

Wuff

Cruncher

Mix and Max and their friends are the science gang. They love finding things out.

You can join in with their finding out games in this book.

My body

Have you got a tail?

Have these animals got tails?

Point to their tails, then colour them red.

Now look at the animals on the next page. On every animal colour each part a different colour.

ears   fingers   eyes
legs   toes   wings

Note to Parents

Playing the game 'Simon says' will help develop your child's knowledge of body parts, e.g. 'Simon says, "Touch your ankle with your thumb."'

Can you name some parts of your body which aren't on the list?

Note to Parents

When your child has coloured the pictures use them to ask questions such as, 'Which animal has got a tail and fur?' or 'Which animal has got a tail but no legs?'

5

My face

Look in a mirror.

How many parts of your face can you name?

What colours are they?

Are they big or small?

I've got small black eyes and big pink ears!

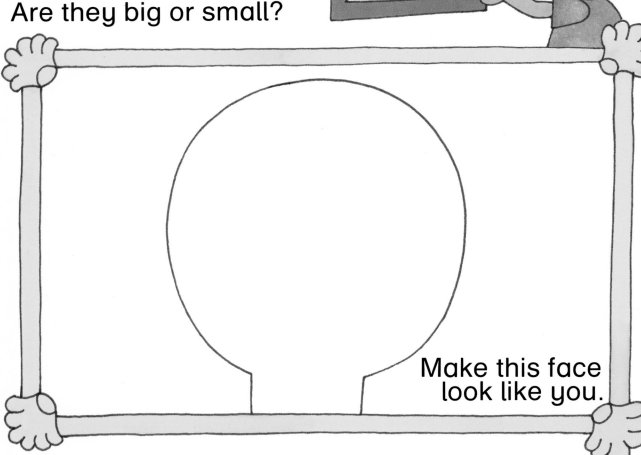

Make this face look like you.

Have you drawn all of these?

eyes

nose

mouth

eyebrows

ears

hair

Draw in anything you have missed out.

Now look in the mirror again. Does your drawing look like you?

6

Look at these pictures.

Can you tell from their faces how Mix and Max are feeling?
Can you see why they feel like this?

Funny face game

Ask a friend or a grown-up to make a face that looks happy, sad, excited, cross or tired. How good are the faces? Can someone guess how you feel when you make a face?

My shadow

Make shadows with your body. You can do it outside on a sunny day or inside with a lamp or a torch.

Can you . . .

. . . make your shadow short and fat?

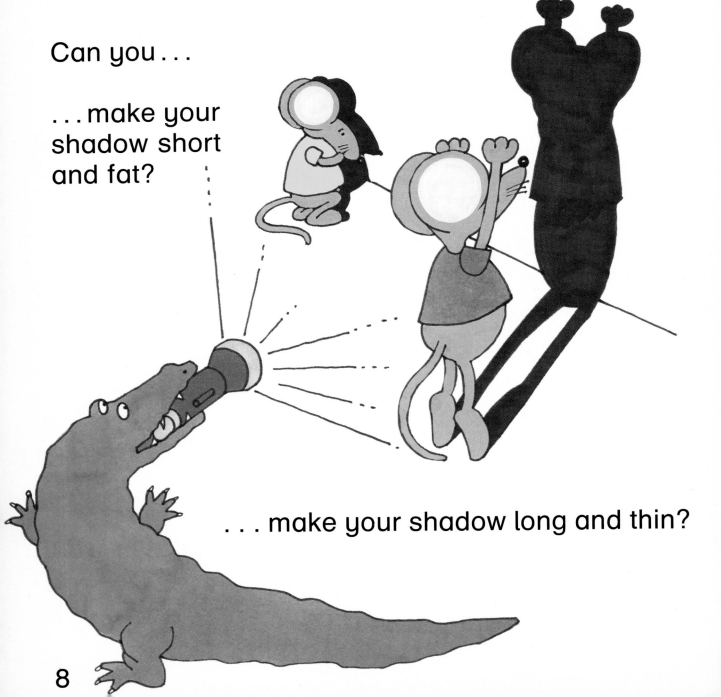

. . . make your shadow long and thin?

8

. . . make a shadow with four arms?

. . . jump on your shadow?

. . . make differently shaped shadows with an umbrella?

9

Smelling

What's that funny smell? Is something burning?

Oh dear! It's the toast.

How good are you at guessing things from their smell? Try this game.

You will need

a friend to play with, some yoghurt pots, a blindfold and some things to smell.
You could try tea, pieces of apple and banana, coffee, fruit, sweets, chocolate, toothpaste and vinegar.

What to do

Put a little of each thing in a yoghurt pot.
Ask your friend to blindfold you. Smell each
pot in turn.

Can you guess what it is?

Tick the things that you guessed first time.

tea ☐   chocolate ☐

apple ☐   toothpaste ☐

coffee ☐   vinegar ☐

_____ ☐   _____ ☐

_____ ☐   _____ ☐

Hearing

Stop and listen carefully. What can **you** hear? Make a list.

_____   _____

_____   _____

_____   _____

_____   _____

Note to Parents
Fill in this list for your child.

BRMM BRMM

BANG BANG

ZZZZZZ

What a lot of noise!
Where is it coming from?

Which of these things can Mix hear?
Tick the right boxes.

Tiger hammering ☐   Owl reading ☐

The sun shining ☐   The birds singing ☐

The fish swimming ☐   Max vacuuming ☐

What else do you think Mix can hear?

My hands

Note to Parents
A family set of hand outlines makes a good wall display.

How big are your hands?
Put one hand on the yellow box and spread
out your fingers. Hold your hand still and
ask a grown-up to draw round it.

Now draw around the grown-up's hand
on a piece of paper.

How much can you hold in one hand?

To find out **you will need** a jug, some marbles, small plastic bricks, dried peas or beans and some sweets.

Put the marbles in the jug. Put one hand into the jug and pick up as many marbles as you can.

Count how many you have picked up.
Write the number in the box.
Then do this again with the other things.

With one hand I can pick up

☐ marbles   ☐ beans

☐ sweets   ☐ bricks

Now ask a grown-up to try picking up these things.

Note to Parents

Ask your child to predict the results of this activity. 'Will you be able to pick up more sweets or more peas?' 'If you can pick up 3 marbles how many do you think I can pick up?'

My feet

Wuff is following footprints on the beach.
Who do you think is behind the rock?
Who is in the hut?

Weather wheel

You will need
one or two friends to play with
1 counter for each player
1 dice

some clothes for
a **wet** day

some clothes for
a **hot** day

some clothes for
a **cold** day

Start

Put back one
thing you have
put on.

How to play

Take turns to throw the dice. Move round the wheel by the number you throw. If you land on a picture of a wet day put on something from the 'wet' pile. Do the same if you land on a hot or cold day. The winner is the first person to be wearing 3 things for the same weather.

Put back one thing you have put on.

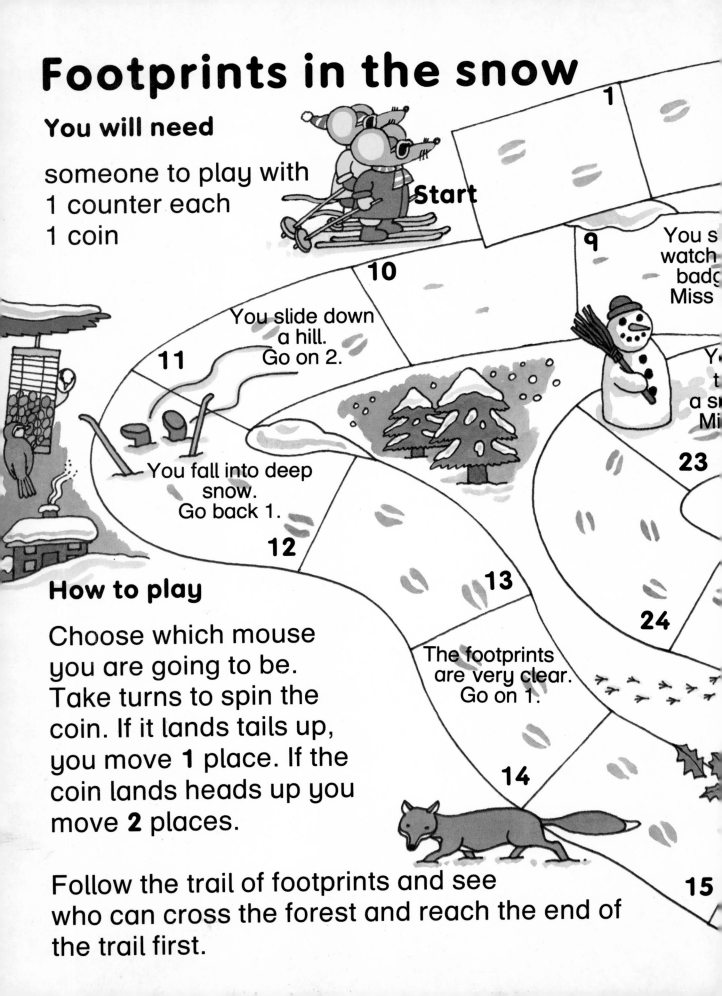

Footprints in the snow

You will need

someone to play with
1 counter each
1 coin

Start

1

9

You s
watch
badg
Miss

10

You slide down
a hill.
Go on 2.

11

You fall into deep
snow.
Go back 1.

Y
t
a s
Mi

23

12

13

24

How to play

Choose which mouse
you are going to be.
Take turns to spin the
coin. If it lands tails up,
you move **1** place. If the
coin lands heads up you
move **2** places.

The footprints
are very clear.
Go on 1.

14

15

Follow the trail of footprints and see
who can cross the forest and reach the end of
the trail first.

What do your footprints look like? To make some **you will need** paper, thick powder or poster paints, a thick paint brush, a bowl of water, an old towel, someone to help.

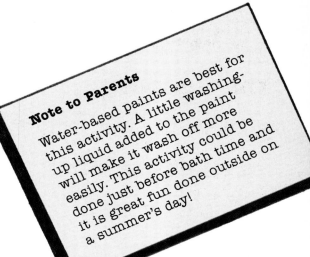

Note to Parents

Water-based paints are best for this activity. A little washing-up liquid added to the paint will make it wash off more easily. This activity could be done just before bath time and it is great fun done outside on a summer's day!

Use the brush to paint the bottom of one foot.

Press the painted foot firmly onto a sheet of paper.

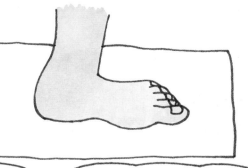

Take someone else's footprint. Is it different from yours?

You can make some patterns!

Cooking

This recipe makes
2 big gingerbread people.

You will need

8 heaped dessertspoons of plain flour
4 heaped dessertspoons of soft brown sugar
120g or 4oz of soft margarine
1 heaped teaspoon of baking powder
1 heaped teaspoon of ground ginger
a little cold water

What to do

1 Wash your hands and put on an apron.
2 Grease a baking tray.
3 Count the spoonfuls of flour, sugar, baking powder and ginger into a large bowl and mix together.
4 Add the margarine and rub into the mixture until it looks like breadcrumbs.
5 Add a little water (2 or 3 dessertspoons should be enough) and use your hands to press the mixture into a ball.

6 Divide the mixture and make 2 people like this.

Make sure your people have a head, 2 arms and 2 legs! Roll out little balls of the mix to make the eyes, nose, mouth and buttons.

7 Put your people on the baking tray and ask a grown-up to put the tray in the oven.
Leave to cook for 20-25 minutes.
Ask a grown-up to take the tray out and leave the gingerbread to cool.

What happened to the gingerbread people while they were in the oven?

_____

_____

Note to Parents

As well as being creative and fun, making gingerbread involves measuring out the ingredients and observing how their properties change as they are mixed and baked. There is no need to roll out the mixture, your child will enjoy moulding it into shape by hand. Before cooking, the people should be at least 1cm (½ inch) thick.

My clothes

The science gang is playing a dressing-up game.

Tiger

Cruncher

Annie

Wuff

Max

Mix

Who do you think is going somewhere hot?

_____ and _____

What is the weather like
where Cruncher is going? _____

What is the weather like where the others
are going?

Which sorts of weather do you think these clothes are for?

Draw lines from each set of clothes to the right weather pictures.

Note to Parents

The classification of weather as hot, cold or wet can be extended to include hot wet weather, cold wet weather, cold sunny weather etc. Discuss how your child might feel if he/she went out dressed for the wrong sort of weather.

Colours

The science gang is watching some fireworks.

I like the red ones. They make everything look warm and cosy.

We like the yellow ones!

What colour fireworks can you see?

My favourite colour is _____

22

Tiger and Owl have saved some clear coloured sweet papers.
They are looking through them.

Everything looks green!

I've made a colour tube to look through.
You can make one too.

You will need

some coloured sweet papers, a toilet roll middle,
some sticky tape and a rubber band.

What to do

Stretch a sweet paper over one end of the tube.
Put on the rubber band and stick the paper in
place with the tape.

Shut one eye and look through the tube.
What can you see?
Try looking at the fireworks. Do their colours
change?

Mix and Max go to the park

Mix and Max are getting ready to go to the park.

Mix is so excited she leaves her breakfast and forgets to clean her teeth.

Max puts on his coat but Mix leaves hers at home.

In the park they meet some friends.

Note to Parents

Use this story to talk about the importance of looking after yourself. 'Why was Mix so tired?' etc.

Read the text under the pictures, then point to the bubbles and read them.

What's wrong with Mix?

I'm cold and hungry. I want to go home.

I wish I had a coat.

Max is having fun but Mix isn't joining in.

On the way home it starts to rain. Mix is wet and miserable.

Time for bed, Mix!

I'll be up later.

Coming, Mix?

No. I'm tired, I've got a cold and my tooth aches. Achoo!

At home in the warm Mix starts to feel better. She stays up late watching TV.

In the morning Max goes to the park again. Mix stays in bed.

25

Moving

Mix and Max usually walk to school...

...but sometimes they run!
Can you see why?

How quickly can you run?   Tick **yes** or **no**.
Are you faster than...

a tortoise?

yes	no

a horse?

yes	no

a deer?

yes	no

a snail?

yes	no

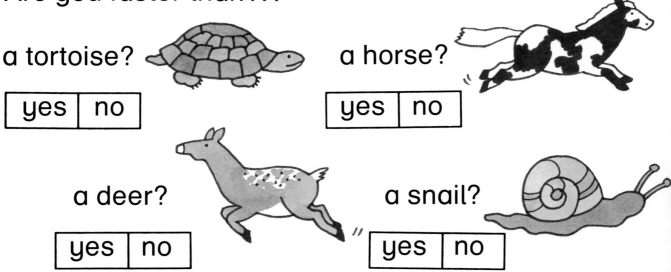

Can you move like these animals?
Tick the box if you can...

jump like a kangaroo

swim like a duck

waddle like a penguin

hop like a rabbit

slither like a snake

Put a star ✳ by the quickest way of moving.

Put a cross ✕ by the most tiring way.

Can you think of other ways to move?

Try them out and write them here.

Note to Parents

Help your child to write the list.
Ways to move might include skipping,
hopping, sliding, galloping, rolling,
shuffling etc. The ways that use most
energy are the most tiring.

Watching and talking about natural
history programmes on TV is a good
way for your child to discover more
about the animal world.

_____

_____

_____

_____

Bath time

Mix and Max are having fun in the bath.
They are playing with the soap, the sponge and
their bath toys.

Try their experiments when you have a bath.

Does the soap float on the water or sink to the bottom? Draw it in the right place.

Does a dry sponge float on the water or sink to the bottom?
Now hold the sponge under water to make it wet.
Draw the dry sponge and the wet sponge in their right places in the bath.

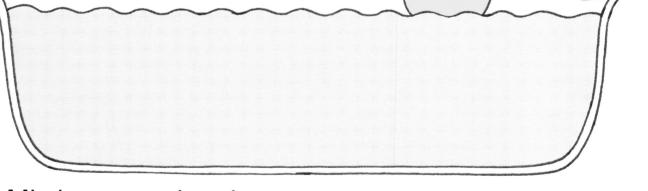

Mix is squeezing the wet sponge over a cup to see how much water comes out.

How much water does your sponge hold?
Tick the right box.

more than a cupful ☐

less than a cupful ☐

Try squeezing an empty plastic shampoo bottle under water.
Does anything come out?

My toys

Mix and Max have made trains to
keep their toys tidy.

Can you make toy trains like Mix and Max?

You will need

some cardboard boxes, felt-tip pens, some toys and some string.

What to do

Ask a grown-up to help you tie the boxes together to make a train. Draw on the wheels and put the driver in the engine.

When your train is ready, load up your toys like Mix has done. Then try loading them like Max.

Can you think of any other ways to load your toys into the train?

Note to Parents

This activity encourages your child to classify objects in a number of ways.

After sorting the toys as hard or soft and old or new your child could sort them as big or small, plastic or not plastic, heavy or light, red or not red, shiny or dull etc. The boxes could be used for sorting other things too, like clothes or books.

More about the ideas in this book

The activities in this book build on children's natural curiosity about themselves and their surroundings, to develop their skills of **observation** and **enquiry**. Children discover the world through their senses – sight, sound, smell, taste and touch. It is important that children are given lots of opportunities to develop their senses and to acquire the language to describe their sensations at an early stage.

Trying out science activities at home will help build your child's confidence and enthusiasm for science at school. In this respect, girls are sometimes at a disadvantage when compared with boys. Girls may lack confidence in their abilities in science simply because they have not been given the same opportunities to play with construction kits or technical toys at home. We hope that both girls and boys will enjoy the activities and start to discover the fun of science.

In all cases the process of **doing** and **enjoying** the activities is much more important than the end result or 'answer' (if indeed there is one!). The most important thing at this early stage in a child's science education is the development of the desire to have a go and see what happens, and the willingness to talk about ideas and discoveries. We hope that together you will have fun discovering science.